美 好 嘅 童 年
CHILDHOOD Is a GREAT JOURNEY

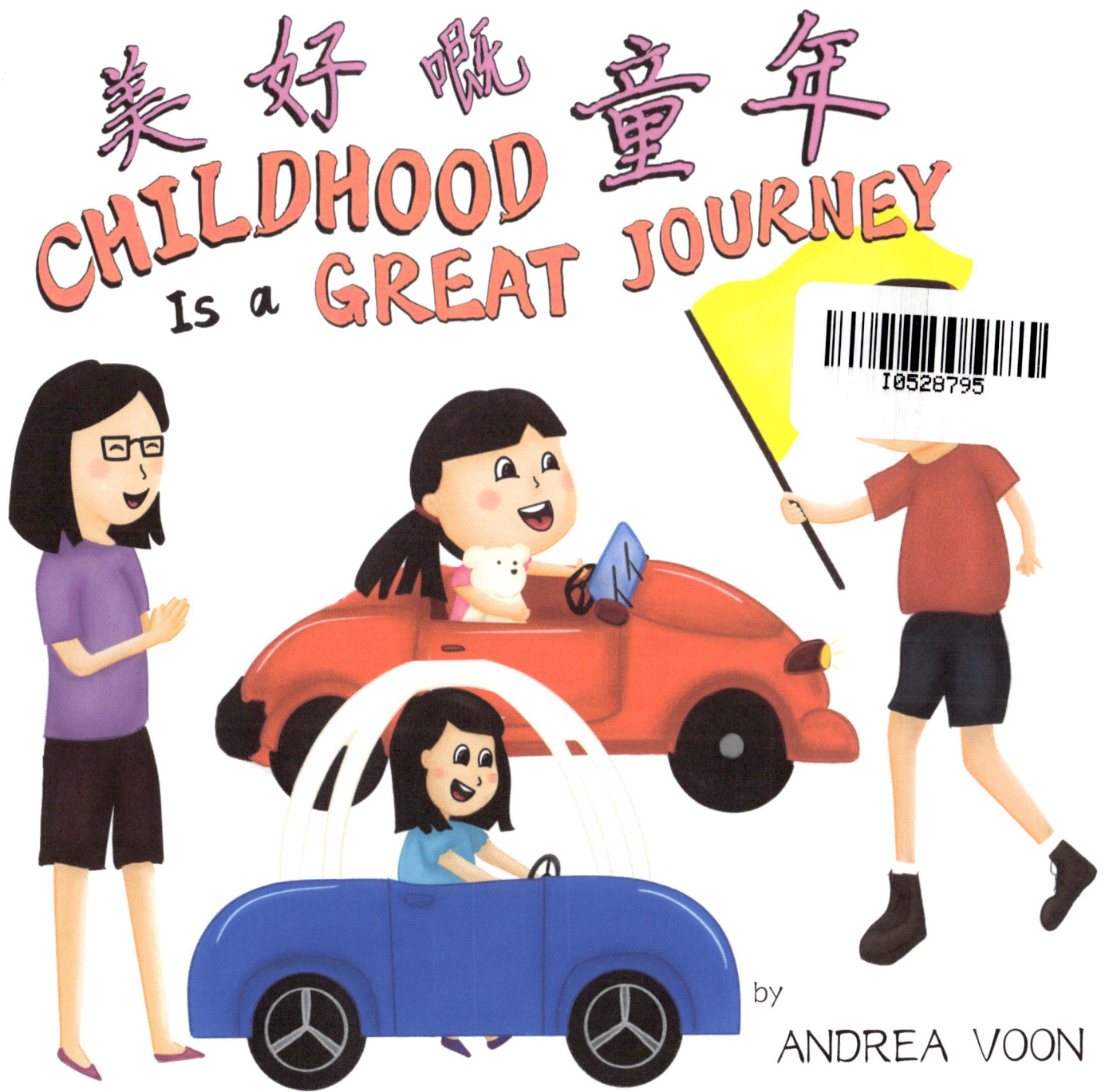

by

ANDREA VOON

好媽咪，請坐低，陪我哋玩煮飯仔。
hou² maa¹ mi⁴ cing² co⁵ dai¹ pui⁴ ngo⁵ dei⁶ waan² zyu² faan⁶ zai²

食乜嘢？慢慢揀，套餐今日大優惠。
sik⁶ mat¹ je⁵ maan⁶ maan² gaan² tou³ caan¹ gam¹ jat⁶ daai⁶ jau¹ wai⁶

凍檸茶，熱咖啡，煎牛扒，烤火雞……
dung³ ning⁴ caa⁴ jit⁶ gaa³ fe¹ zin¹ ngau⁴ paa² haau¹ fo² gai¹

食甜品，送雪糕，蛋糕好食又好睇。
sik⁶ tim⁴ ban² sung³ syut³ gou¹ daan⁶ gou¹ hou² sik⁶ jau⁶ hou² tai²

Hot soup? **Cooked**. Turkey? **Cooked**.
Let's preheat the big oven,
and bake a birthday cake.

Tea and coffee... Cupcakes and ice creams...
we're ready for a tea party
when mummy takes her break.

洗切煮炒好手勢， 甜酸苦辣啱口味。

sai² cit³ zyu² caau² hou² sau² sai³　tim⁴ syun¹ fu² laat⁶ ngaam¹ hau² mei⁶

愛心餸菜最開胃， 食得健康唔怕肥。

oi³ sam¹ sung³ coi³ zeoi³ hoi¹ wai⁶　sik⁶ dak¹ gin⁶ hong¹ m⁴ paa³ fei⁴

Washing and cooking while sipping on our milkshake.

Eating and laughing until we have a stomach ache.

4

左手輕，右手重，黑鍵、白鍵叮叮響。

左邊壓，右邊掃，高音、低音輕輕揚。

彈鋼琴，彈吉他，揸住支咪高聲唱。

拍拍手，踏踏腳，唱完一場又一場。

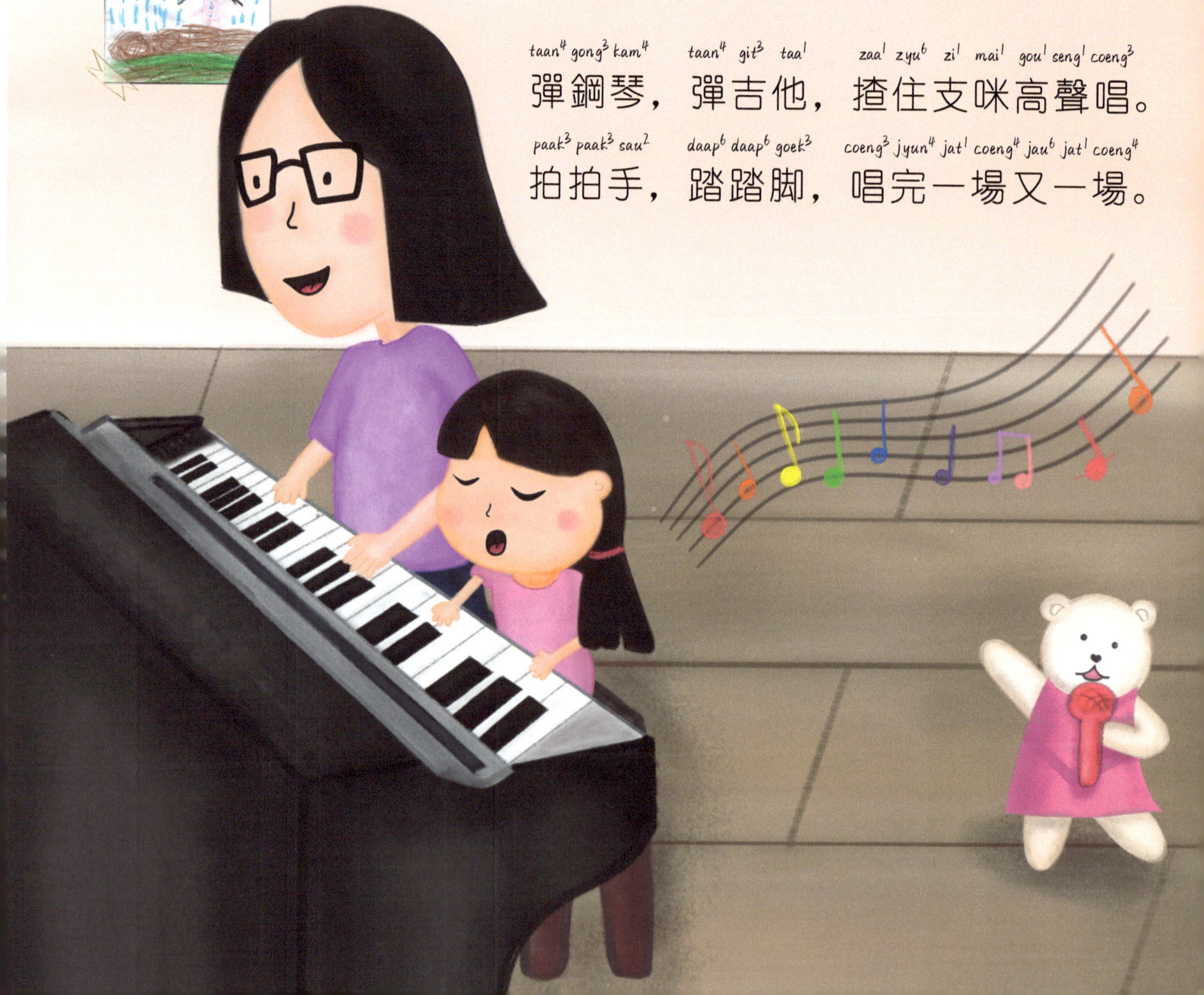

White keys, black keys... Do-re-mi-fa-so-
Let's form a music band, and play our favorite song.
High notes, low notes... So-fa-mi-re-do-
Tapping and clapping, and repeat all day long.

haau¹ tung⁴ bat⁶   daa² lo⁴ gu²   baa¹ leoi⁵ mou⁵ kwan⁴ tam⁴ tam² zyun³

敲銅鈸， 打鑼鼓， 芭蕾舞裙冰冰轉。

sau² laai¹ sau²   zyun³ hyun¹ hyun¹   coeng³ coeng³ tiu³ tiu³ hei³ m⁴ cyun²

手拉手， 轉圈圈， 唱唱跳跳氣唔喘。

One, two, three, four...
Sing our happy song loud and strong.

Move it... Groove it...
Skip around a circle, and dance along.

Tweezers? **Set!** Bandages? **Set!**

Daddy sprained his ankle in a soccer game.

Stethoscope? **Cleaned!** Thermometer? **Cleaned!**

We're ready for the next patient, **PLEASE** call out her name.

急診室，多病人，請你耐心等一陣。

量血壓，探下熱，醫生輪住嚟睇診。

爹地唔小心扭親，隻腳嚴重傷到筋。

打支針，再包紮，后日記得嚟覆診。

親親妹妹作感冒，又屙又嘔頭暈暈。

can¹ can¹ mui⁴ mui² zok³ gam² mou⁶　jau⁶ o¹ jau⁶ au² tau⁴ wan⁴ wan⁴

食完藥，飲啖水，瞓醒就會好精神。

sik⁶ jyun⁴ joek⁶　jam² daam⁶ seoi²　fan³ seng² zau⁶ wui⁵ hou² zing¹ san⁴

Here are your medicines,
PLEASE drink more water.

Take a good bed rest,
and you'll be better.

媽咪揸住購物單，帶埋我哋去行街。

maa¹ mi⁴ zaa¹ zyu⁶ kau³ mat⁶ daan¹ daai³ maai⁴ ngo⁵ dei⁶ heoi³ haang⁴ gaai¹

推車仔，來掃貨，睇下有乜嘢好買。

teoi¹ ce¹ zai² loi⁴ sou³ fo³ tai² haa⁵ jau⁵ mat¹ je⁵ hou² maai⁵

Oranges? **Yes**! Apples? **No**!
Let's be a smart helper
at the mini-mart.

gaan² seoi² gwo²　　gaan² ling⁴ sik⁶　　ngo⁵ tung⁴ mui⁴ mui² loi⁴ dau³ faai³

揀水果，揀零食，我同妹妹來鬥快。

tai² zat¹ dei²　　tai² gaa³ cin⁴　　bin¹ go³ paai⁴ zi² ho² seon³ laai⁶

睇質地，睇價錢，邊個牌子可信賴？

Cookies? **Here**! Fresh milk? **There**!

we're ready for the checkout
with a heavy cart.

san¹ wun⁶ geoi⁶　　hou² paai⁴ zi²　　peng⁴ leng³ zeng³　　sin¹ dai² maai⁵

新玩具，好牌子，平靚正，先抵買。

jat¹ baak³ man¹　　m⁴ sai² zaau²　　daai⁶ maai⁶ dak⁶ maai⁶ zan¹ tung³ faai³

一百蚊，唔使找，大賣特賣真痛快。

Which toy is cheaper?
Which treat is tastier?

One hundred dollars,
and **THANK YOU**, dear cashier.

lok6 daai6 jyu5 gwaat3 daai6 fung1 daai6 gaa1 ci1 maai4 waan2 jau4 hei3

落大雨，颳大風，大家黐埋玩游戲。

jat1 gaa1 jan4 jiu3 wo4 hei3 m4 zaang1 syu1 jeng4 m4 dau3 hei3

一家人，要和氣，唔爭輸贏唔鬥氣。

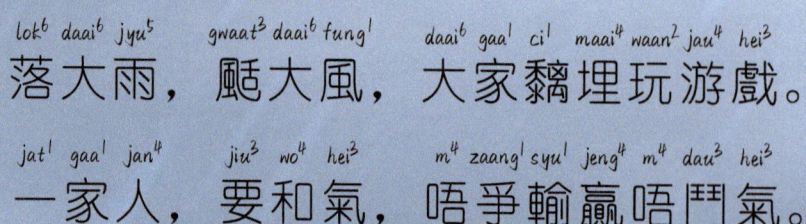

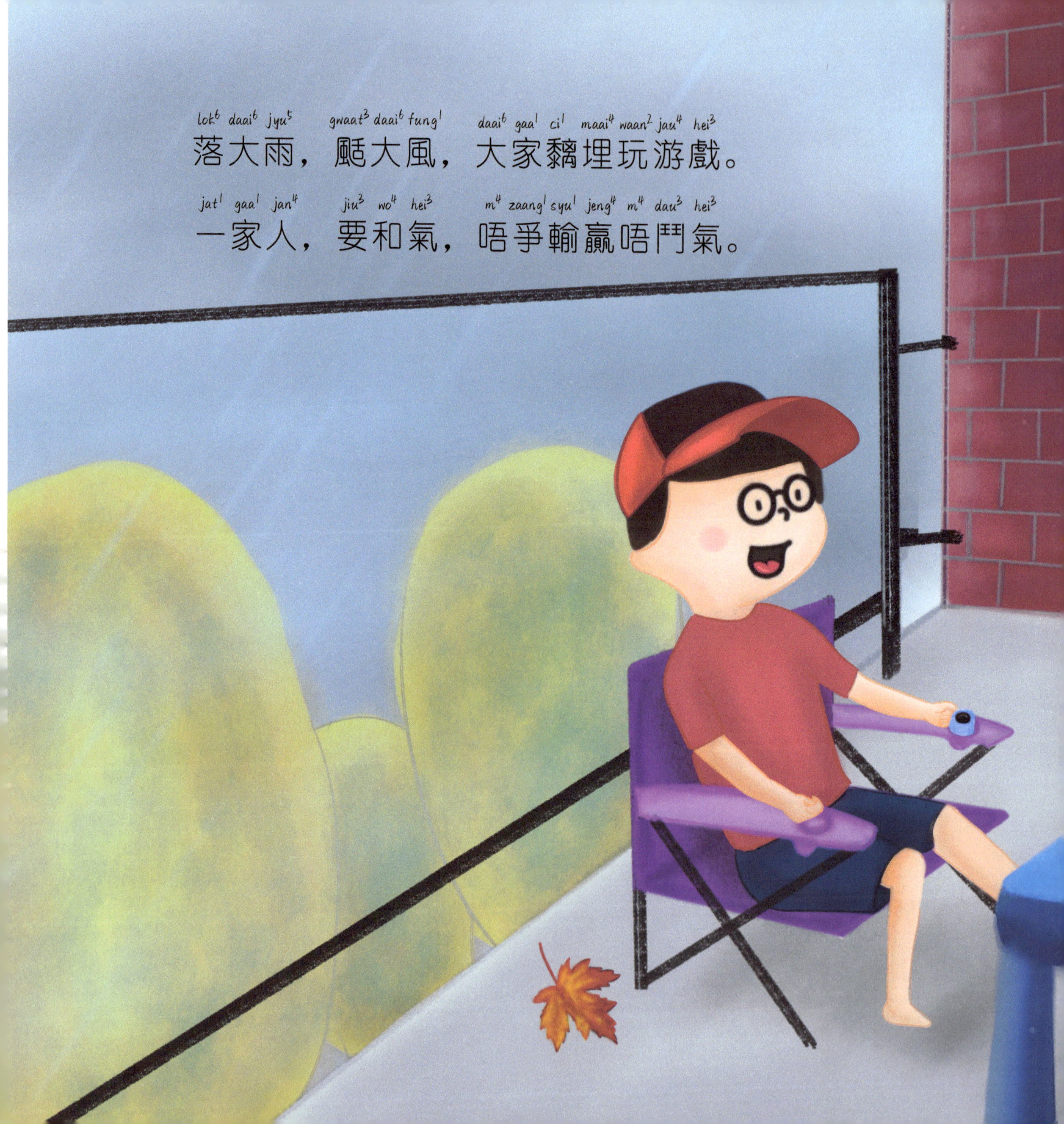

Red or yellow; Green or blue?
Let's choose a fun game to kick-start our date.

Whose turn is it now? Who is the winner?

The sky is gloomy, yet we're doing **GREAT!**

fan³ gaau³ cin⁴　jiu³ caat³ ngaa⁴　laan⁶ ngaa⁴ m⁴ wui⁵ cin⁴ zyu⁶ nei⁵

瞓覺前，要刷牙，爛牙唔會纏住你。

kam² hou² pei⁵　sek³ faan¹ daam⁶　ok³ mung⁶ m⁴ wui⁵ cin⁴ zyu⁶ nei⁵

冚好被，錫翻啖，噩夢唔會纏住你。

Up and down, in and out...
Brush your little teeth twice a day.

CAVITIES! Keep at bay!
Call it a day, and hit the hay.

企直直，咪亂啷，身高體重要記低。

量一量，磅一磅，睇吓你哋乖唔乖。

唔揀食，唔曳曳，爹地媽咪就錫晒。

眨吓眼，就長大，時間過得真係快。

Veggies and fruits; Eggs and meats.
I'm **NOT** picky, and I clean up my plate!

Did I grow taller? Did I get **heavier**?
As tall as Mum and Dad! I just **CAN'T** wait!

背書包，去返學，面帶笑容講拜拜。

me¹ syu¹ baau¹ heoi³ faan¹ hok⁶ min⁶ daai³ siu³ jung⁴ gong² baai¹ baai³

招招手，攬一攬，開開心心唔扭計。

ziu¹ ziu¹ sau² laam⁵ jat¹ laam⁵ hoi¹ hoi¹ sam¹ sam¹ m⁴ nau² gai²

Lunch box? **Checked**!

Backpack? **Checked**!

"**HOORAY** for school!"

Teddy cheers.

Goodbye, Mom!
Goodbye, Dad!
Goodbye, little sis!
Shed **NO** tears!

美好嘅童年，
mei⁵ hou² ge³ tung⁴ nin⁶

有屋企人喺身邊，
jau⁵ uk¹ kei² jan⁴ hai² san¹ bin¹

齊玩樂，齊歡笑。
cai⁴ wun⁶ lok⁶ cai⁴ fun¹ siu³

CHILDHOOD is a great journey,

together with you,
we create lasting memories.

作者 Author

溫甘玉芬

當媽前，她是孩子們的甘老師，在常年暖和的熱帶雨林，與孩子一起學習中、英文，探索文字的奧秘；當媽後，她是孩子們的溫媽咪，在四季分明的北半球，與孩子一起感受春夏秋冬的更替，一起尋找美好的童年……

溫媽咪創作的靈感，源自於多年來的童言童語。

2021年，她成立了"溫室工作坊"，立志出版一系列的中、英雙語繪本，結合母語和第二語言，提倡親子趣讀。精通三語的溫媽咪理解每一種語言都有其獨特的藝術形式，因此創作的雙語繪本也各含韻味、各具特色。

Andrea Voon

Over the past few years, Andrea has learned and grown with her family as a full-time mother in Canada. Back in Malaysia, she worked as a teacher in Chinese immersion elementary school. In 2021, Andrea started her journey as a self-publisher. Growing up in a multilingual environment, Andrea loves the beauty of languages on their own. She has the vision to publish picture books to support bilingual families in raising their children in English and Chinese reading.

To Derek, Eliana, Alayna & Magnus Dominus
with love -- Andrea V.

備註：繪本中的"壁畫"源自溫室工作坊各成員的手作。

p/s: "Pictures on the wall" in this book are special art collection of

HEI Greenhouse Studio's members.

Check out other bilingual picture books by Andrea Voon.

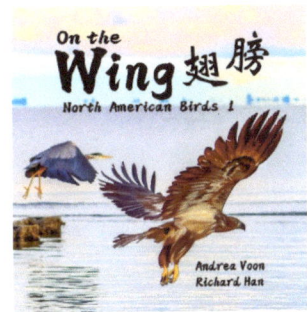
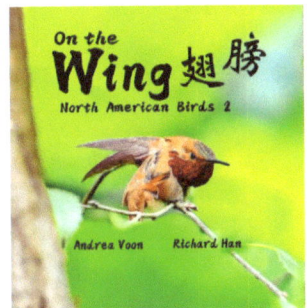
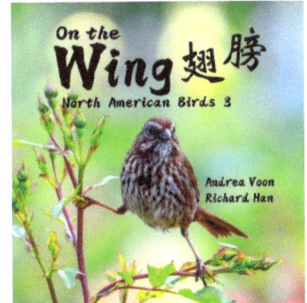

双语阅读，乐趣无穷！
BILINGUAL READING IS FUN!

ISBN 978-1-998856-00-8
Text copyright © by 2024 Andrea Voon.
Illustration copyright © 2024 Andrea Voon, Yapp Shin Enn.

温室工作坊